TIBET

JOURNEY TO THE FORBIDDEN CITY

Retracing the steps of Alexandra David-Néel

Tiziana and Gianni Baldizzone

STEWART, TABORI & CHANG

NEW YORK

Contents

Text and photographs by:
Tiziana and Gianni Baldizzone

Edited by:
Valeria Manferto De Fabianis

Designed by:
Patrizia Balocco Lovisetti

Translated by:
Ann Hylands Ghiringhelli

© 1994 White Star S.r.l.
Via Candido Sassone, 24
13100 Vercelli, Italy

Published in 1996 and distributed in the U.S. by
Stewart, Tabori & Chang,
a division of U.S. Media Holdings, Inc.
575 Broadway, New York, NY 10012

Library of Congress Catalog Card Number 96-68049

ISBN: 1-55670-511-5

Printed in Italy

10 9 8 7 6 5 4 3 2 1

The authors wish to thank: the government authorities of Sichuan and Qinghai; their Tibetan friends in Kham and Amdo; Marie Madeleine Peyronnet and Frank Treguier of the Fondation A. David-Néel; Ge Shi Dong and family; Tsa Tsa Lama Chang Chub Dorjié and Morena Rossi; Carla Milone; Paola Renegaldo; Ernesto Lo Bue. Thanks also go to Europhoto and T.T.P. Tardivello photographic services for their technical support.
NOTE: Passages in inverted commas are not precise quotations from Alexandra David-Néel's books but paraphrases from the original French editions; for sources see page 160.

Alexandra David-Néel (1868-1969) was the first great female traveler and journalist of the twentieth century. At a time when women were still brought up to consider marriage and motherhood their only vocations in life, she turned her back on convention and her native city of Paris to travel to remote parts of the Far East, Central Asia and other continents. A born traveler, she told journalists who pestered her with questions that she would even have embarked on a journey simply to "put one foot in front of the other." The main objective of her expeditions was research into ethnography, philosophy and religion. When she set out for the Far East in 1911, fired by a profound spiritual need, she planned to spend only eighteen months there. She in fact returned after thirteen years, bringing with her an amazing record of her life and travels in the form of about 3000 photographs. These she used to illustrate the accounts of her experiences that won her a place of honor among orientalist explorers. One regret, as she told her husband in a letter in 1911-12, was "that photography cannot convey the true colors of this wonderful Land of Snows...."

Preface

The great progress made in photography since the time of its pioneer, Nicéphore Niepce, has now enabled Tiziana and Gianni Baldizzone to record their own travels with the outstanding photographs presented here. Journeying across Kham in the footsteps of Alexandra David-Néel, they captured their experiences in stunning images, in ravishing color. They then had the idea of placing them alongside Alexandra David-Néel's black-and-white photos of this starkly beautiful province. The result would have brought great joy to an exceptional woman. Even just before her death, close to her 101st birthday, she was still relating her adventures in the immensity of Kham, which she affectionately called the "Land of the Gentlemen Brigands!"

Marie Madeleine Peyronnet
Fondation Alexandra David-Néel

"**G**entlemen brigands" is how Alexandra David-Néel described the inhabitants of the regions in the far west of China which she crossed in 1920-21 in her first expedition to Lhasa. She was determined to reach the "Forbidden City" at any cost, evading the notice of the Tibetan authorities. Accompanied by Yongden, the young lama (religious teacher) who was her inseparable traveling companion—and later her adopted son—she ventured into territories inhabited by nomadic peoples who were reportedly fierce brigands, given to plundering the caravans that made their way to Lhasa from China. Her journey was not only a challenge: she saw it also as a unique opportunity to travel along unexplored trails; to indulge her fascination with the wild nature of the vast solitudes of the plateaux; and to learn more about the peoples of the tablelands and their traditions and beliefs, rooted in mysticism and magic. Explorer, writer, orientalist, anchorite in a Himalayan cave and lecturer in Paris, operasinger and lama, accepted by the local people as a *khadoma* ("sky-goer:" a kind of female genie whom Tibetans believe can sometimes be incarnated in our own

Introduction

world), Alexandra David-Néel succeeded in traveling through the forbidden enclave. The image of eastern Tibet she conveyed to the outside world was a very particular one, for she presented the region in a different light from other Western travelers who visited it before or after her. In her accounts of her travels and in her stories, the detailed, colorful descriptions of places and of the everyday lives of local people are indissolubly linked with the mysterious and the transcendent that pervade every aspect of Tibetan existence. As a lama herself, Alexandra David-Néel was aware of all the manifestations of mysticism; and her Western cultural background enabled her to analyze them logically and rationally.

Retracing the steps of Alexandra David-Néel

From the very first reading of her book we were fascinated by her account of the Kham country, partly because it was an untamed wilderness, but mostly because it was the home of the Khampa, a people of forbidding appearance, obscure origins and intimidating reputation. Tales told by early Western explorers had made their name a byword for robbery and plunder. But it was later also linked with courage and heroism, for the Khampa were instigators and leaders of Tibetan resistance to the Chinese. For over a decade, they fought in the name of their independence and their Buddhist faith, fired by the spirit of freedom that always made them a race apart. Like Alexandra David-Néel, we too felt an irresistible urge to roam the vast spaces of the Land of Snows; we too were interested in the culture of the groups who populate the region. We also wanted to discover which aspects of the eastern Tibet she described still survived in regions that had been the scene of bloody fighting at the time of the Cultural Revolution and now, with improved communications, are far less isolated. Seventy years after Alexandra David-Néel, we ventured in search of the Gentlemen Brigands, using her writings as our map and guide.

This book is not a personal story, nor does it set out to provide an exhaustive account of the geography, history, culture and religion of eastern Tibet. It is a kind of journey between past and present, following an ideal itinerary that introduces the reader to places where the nomad peoples encountered by Alexandra David-Néel lived, and still live today. It is also the story of the boundless solitudes where she spent much time lost in meditation, of the history and traditions of a proud and spirited people, and of the religious and spiritual aspects of the "Land of the Gentlemen Brigands." A land which, although partly situated outside the geographical borders of Tibet, belongs essentially to Tibetan culture and tradition.

"Twice I departed in secret, as dawn broke, leading my small caravan across the immense Tibetan solitudes; barren deserts and grassland deserts, equally silent, wild, mysterious; harsh, dramatic uplands, realm of dreams, terra incognita...."[1] Shrouded in a blanket of cloud in the early hours of a summer day, the grassy plains of Amdo contain all the fascination and mystery of eastern Tibet, a never-ending wilderness of empty, wind-swept spaces. There is no shelter, no barrier but the surrounding mountains. The unbounded grassy steppes reveal no sign of human life. Silence is absolute—overwhelming and impressive. Solitude is allen compassing, holding travelers in its frightening grasp. Tibetan in terms of culture and ethnic groups but—as in the time of Alexandra David-Née—part of the Chinese provinces of Qinghai and Sichuan, these eastern regions are perhaps the most secret part of Tibet (*Bodh Po* in Tibetan, meaning "high land"). Their elevation, rugged mountain ranges and reputedly fierce populations have made access difficult and contributed to their continuing mystery and enchantment. The country is a geographical fortress—with vast spaces guarded by

Nomads of the Grassland Deserts

huge mountain masses from the Himalaya to the Anye Machin, a severe climate, uninviting terrain, such as the Chang Tang plateau, and untamed peoples like the Lolo, who dwell in valleys close to the Chinese border. The isolation of the eastern regions has been increased by tales about their barbarous, aggressive inhabitants. Fear of attack and robbery made the few Western travelers who crossed central Asia careful not to pass this way.

*Born nomads and brigands, the peoples of Kham and Amdo are now
essentially shepherds and herders of animals, above all yaks. On the
previous pages: left, a portrait of Alexandra David-Néel in traveling
clothes; right, a Khampa woman with the typical hairstyle of braided locks
(Nyarong).*

From Marco Polo to Odoric of Pordenone, from Jesuit and Franciscan missionaries to British expeditions sent to Lhasa from India, all followed routes which, except for occasional sallies into the region, kept well away from eastern Tibet. Western travelers began to penetrate the area towards the end of the 1800s, when expeditions of explorers arrived from China or the northern part of Vietnam. The Tibetans themselves regarded the inhabitants of the eastern territories as barbarians, their lands crossed by the caravans that traveled the

Sichuan ("land of the four rivers"). The most notable feature of this region—and Amdo especially—is its immenseness: what Alexandra David-Néel described as an "empty" green landscape of grass and lakes.

The province is named after the great Lake Qinghai, which in Mongolian (Kokonor) and Tibetan (Tso Niompo) is the "blue lake," venerated by nomads who consider it the dwelling place of the Naga, powerful water-gods. Alexandra David-Néel reported that no vessel was allowed to sail on its waters because

"tea road" from Lhasa to Kangding, formerly Tachienlu, in Sichuan. In 1950 the same road was used by the Chinese to invade Tibet.

The vast grassy plateaux of Amdo and Kham, furrowed by deep valleys, extend into the modern Chinese provinces of Qinghai (meaning "green sea") and

"according to the natives, the magical spirits which live on the bottom of the lake, in palaces of crystal and gold, would take offense if shadows of boats were cast over their dwellings."[2]

Amdo is a world of boundless grasslands where even animal life is rare. The peoples who live here (Amdowa, Golok,

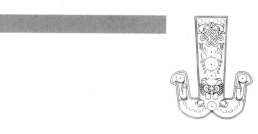

"… the immense Tibetan solitudes; barren deserts and grassland deserts,
equally silent, wild, mysterious; harsh, dramatic uplands, realm of dreams,
terra incognita…"[1]

Mongols) are little known and were once independent of the government in Lhasa, as well as of the Chinese. The Tibetans called them *thapas*, meaning people of "the extremities" or distant frontiers—in other words, barbarians.

The native populations of the plateaux of eastern Tibet are of varying origin. The Amdowa, Khampa and Golok peoples are indigenous to the region. The Mongol communities settled here in the thirteenth century. Nomad warriors of Genghis Khan, they drove out the original inhabitants, the Qiang, who took refuge in the deep valleys of Sichuan.

Few parts of the globe are better suited to pasturage than eastern Tibet. Some of the people of Amdo and Kham are *dokpa*, "people of the solitudes," herders who live a nomadic existence in their tents on the plateaux. Others, the *rongdok* or *dokyul* (from the Tibetan words: *rong*, valley; *dok*, solitude; *yul*, country or village), have adopted an intermediate lifestyle: farmers in the valleys for much of the year, and herders in the high pastures during summer. As Alexandra David-Néel explained, "the real *dokpa* has a genuine horror of houses, because it terrifies him to have a roof between himself and the sky."[3]

From inside his tent a *dokpa* can see the sky through the *kung* (the word means "sky"), a large smoke-hole in the top of the tent, closed only in the event of heavy rain or snowfalls. There is a *kung* in every tent, whether it be the sturdy, circular yurt of the Mongols—consisting

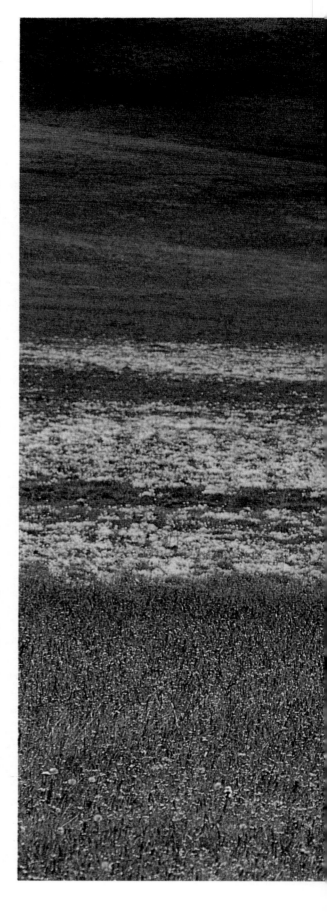

of felt stretched over a collapsible wooden framework—or the low, black tent, firmly secured to the ground by a myriad of twisted yak-hair ropes, made to withstand strong winds. Tents such as these were described by Friar Odoric of Pordenone in his account of a journey through the region in 1328. Each tent is guarded by fierce Tibetan mastiffs, the nomads' faithful companions, who bark furiously to warn of the presence of intruders.

We make our approach to one camp almost in slow-motion, as though respecting some kind of ritual. Ready to pounce, the dogs guard their territory, creating an invisible barrier between us and the nomads. Sangpo, an old *dokpa* of imposing build, wrapped in a thick sheepskin garment which leaves one of his shoulders free, has been watching us from the entrance to his tent. He now comes towards us and has the dogs tied up. In front of the tent two young women with bright red cheeks are twisting long yak hairs on large wooden spools to make rope. Bent over a low loom fixed into the ground, another is weaving yak hair into long strips of black cloth, about 30 cm (12 in) wide. Sewn together, these form the tough, waterproof material used to make tents.

Nearby, a woman is busy making butter in an old wooden churn. Milk is the nomads' main source of nourishment. The yak cow, called *dri*, provides milk all year round. The *dokpa* turn much of the milk into yogurt and butter, stored in

Two nomads ride across the grassy plains of Amdo which, in summer, are
carpeted with flowers. Herbs, roots, resins, flowers and minerals have
always been basic elements in the pharmacopoeia used in Tibetan medicine,
made famous by the seventeenth-century treatise of Sangye Gyamtso.

Every morning, when the men take the herds to pasture, the women remain
at the campsite. Their main tasks are gathering dung, which is then dried
for fuel, and spinning and weaving yak hair to make cloth for dra, the
nomads' traditional black tents.

sacks made from goats' stomachs and used when fresh milk runs short, towards the end of winter. After separating the butter from the yogurt, the remaining liquid is boiled and turned into white curds. Dried in the sun until rock-hard, this cheese serves as reserve provisions that can be kept for years.

With a welcoming gesture, Sangpo leads the way to the tent. Greetings are followed by the customary questions: where do we come from; what brings us to his tent; what news do we bring? Among inhabitants of the grassy deserts offering hospitality to passing travelers is almost a duty. But before allowing

strangers into the tent, the focal point of camp life, it is as well—says our host—to make sure their intentions are friendly. This wary attitude towards strangers may stem from ancestral notions—mentioned by Alexandra David-Néel—that they may unwittingly be harboring some evil demon which will thus gain entrance. Once over the threshold, facing south and therefore thought to bring good luck, we are accommodated on the right-hand side of the tent, reserved for men and guests. Inside, in the cosy darkness of the smoky interior, every item has its own special place, allotted by traditional customs and beliefs. All day-to-day needs are provided for: on the west side are butter, yogurt, *tsampa* and a store of yak dung, used as fuel; on the east side, saddles, swords, guns, wooden boxes and bags made of yak hide or sheepskin in which the men carry their personal belongings and provisions when they take their herds to pasture.

Seated on their respective sides of the tent—male and female—two nomads from Kham (Shaluli Shan area) warm themselves with a bowl of typical Tibetan tea, made with salt and butter. The photo of two young Khampa, opposite, was taken by Alexandra David-Néel.

The long clay fireplace beneath the smoke-hole separates the men's side of the tent from the women's. Nomads believe the prosperity of people and animals is safeguarded in this area. Here food is prepared and preserved, with the exception of meat, which can be handled only on the male side.

An old woman with long braided hair, her face seemingly carved with wrinkles, busies herself preparing buttered tea. This is an age-old ritual that all travelers to Tibet have occasion to witness. With a knife she cuts a piece from a large brick of compressed tea from China, and then chops it into smaller pieces; she boils the tea for a long time and adds salt and butter. Before serving it, she sprinkles a few drops in the direction of the *kung*, to invoke the goodwill of the gods.

Lhamo, the young weaver, has meanwhile returned to the tent and begins to prepare *tsampa*, which is made from roasted barley ground into flour with a stone hand-mill. The nomads' diet is far from varied and *tsampa* is their staple food: stirred into water or tea, or mixed with butter, it is both filling and nourishing. Blue smoke drifts slowly towards the *kung* and in the rear and most sacred part of the tent, the old *dokpa* places a piece of gauze over her mouth, before opening a painted chest in which sacred

images of Buddha and the Dalai Lama are kept. She lights a small butter lamp. "Are you married? How many children can you have in your country?" enquires Lhamo, filling our bowl with tea again. Lhamo is twenty-two and, even after marriage, still lives with her father, together with her husband. This was arranged—she explains—as part of the pre-matrimonial agreement between the two families: Lhamo's household had fewer members and men were needed to take the herds to pasture.

For nomads, marriage rites begin with a meeting between the two families to settle the matrimonial terms: the number of yaks to be contributed by the father of the groom; the jewels to be offered by the bride as her dowry—amber, corals, turquoises and jewelry like the silver hook, studded with coral and turquoise, originally used to secure the milking bucket to prevent the yaks kicking it over. A very wise lama, consulted by Lhamo's father, had sought advice from the gods and from almanacs to decide on a date for the wedding that augured well for the marriage. Lhamo had then spent three days with the family of her future bridegroom, making herself known to relations and guests. At dawn on the wedding day, in her own family's tent, she prepared to greet her bridegroom.

The origins of the Khampa tribes remain a mystery: some say they descend from Qiang peoples; according to legend, they are descended from the ancient inhabitants of the "land of the rock-demons."

The kung is a smoke-hole in the roof of the tent; a few drops of tea or yogurt are sprinkled in its direction to invoke the favor of the kungla, deities of the heavens (Kham).

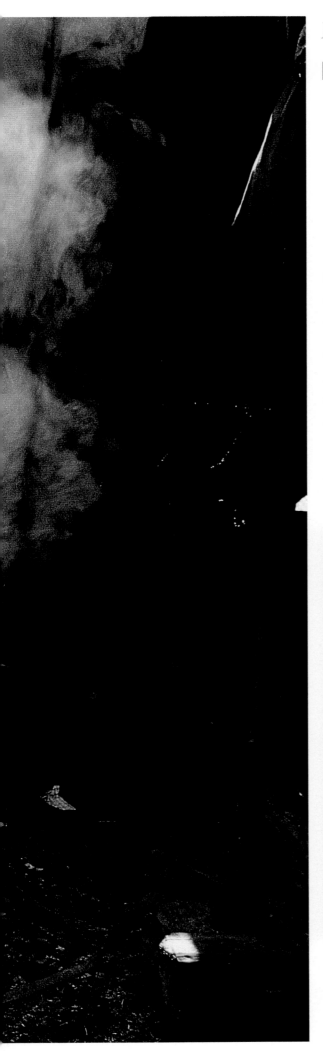

Lhamo's hair, tied in the traditional 108 braids, was fixed to a wide band, woven with corals and turquoises. She wore a brocade robe, trimmed with marmotfur, and silver and turquoise jewelry. The groom arrived escorted by his brother. On horseback, the couple then left for the tent of the groom's family. Here Lhamo was welcomed by a young girl who presented her with a pink scarf to place over her mouth and ears and, taking the horse

drops skywards, invoking the protection of Buddha and the mountain deities. Known as the "offering of the yogurt oath," this is the most important of the marriage rites.

Nomads and brigands, the peoples of the grassy deserts are essentially herdsmen. The characteristic feature of the *dokpa* way of life is not the fact that they live in tents, but rather their complete dependence on the herds they rear. They

by its reins, led her to the tent. A red carpet—red is an auspicious color for weddings—had been placed on the ground where she dismounted.

Once inside the tent, Lhamo was given a bowl of yogurt. With the ring finger of her right hand she had sprinkled a few

are constantly on the move—from summer pastures (*yarsa*) to winter ones (*yunsa*)—to meet their herds' need for fresh grazing. Their survival depends on their animals, which, according to an old saying should number "ten thousand sheep and one thousand yaks."

*Firmly secured by numerous yak-hair ropes, the nomads' black tent has
four sides and a roof reaching down to the ground; close to the entrance is
the hearth, focal point of family life (Lake Kokonor, Amdo).*

"Among the dokpa, some are Mongols.... The Mongol tent has a
collapsible structure made of fairly thin wood. This circular framework...is
covered with felt cloth."[4]

Their goats are of the cashmere breed, from which comes the finest quality wool, taken to collection centers at the end of the summer. The yak is a unique creature they could not live without. A pack and saddle animal, it is docile and ideal for elderly people and children; it is hardier than a mule and sure-footed on almost impracticable paths. Accustomed over the centuries to the high elevation and severe climate of these regions, it is perfectly able to withstand the harsh winters. Its thick coat supplies hair to make tents, blankets, bags and ropes; warm clothing is made from the wool which falls in summer from the soft undercoat of its belly; its meat and milk are tasty and nutritious; its skin and hide are used for blankets and clothes; even its tail serves a purpose as a fly whisk. Gathered from around the camp each morning and left to dry, yak dung is still the only available fuel in these treeless regions at such high altitudes.

When the sun disappears behind the mountains, the echoing songs of the *dokpa* can be heard as they make their way back to the camp with the *dri* (the male yaks are often left in the open pastures). They arrive on horseback or on foot, turning a wooden spindle between their fingers, with which they spin yak hair into thread.

When describing the natives of Amdo, Alexandra David-Néel admitted that— seen close-up, naked underneath their

long, greasy sheepskin coats—they did indeed perhaps look like barbarians. But, when "viewed from a distance, their appearance changes. The grease ingrained in their sheepskin garment, worn with the wool next to the skin, gives it a bronze finish like olive or dark-brown velvet. Sitting erect in the saddle, with a sword in an ornate silver-and-coral sheath stuck in their belt and a gun slung over their shoulder, these coarse-looking men—of fine stature and haughty bearing — are transformed into splendid horsemen."[5]

Supper is the main meal of the day and it is a time when the whole family gathers around the fire, talking, joking and discussing the day's events. Outside the tent, darkness has now descended. Our hosts' voices grow softer and sleepier; their faces become flickering shadows in the fading light of the dying embers.

Alexandra David-Néel described these same deserts of grass and her feelings towards them in a letter to her husband, written more than seventy years ago. "Sensuality is something each one of us experiences according to our own sensibility; in my own case it is related to solitude, silence, virgin lands revealing no sign of cultivation, wide open spaces and the rough life, under canvas, of the nomads of Central Asia."[6]

A Mongol woman disassembles the yurt; hanging from her waist is a traditional hook-shaped silver ornament, originally used to secure the milking bucket (Henan).

Skilled craftsmen create the jewelry traditionally worn by the Khampa and Amdowa peoples. In the picture opposite, a young bride wears her hair in time-honoured fashion, divided into 108 braids held together at the ends by a band—in one of an assortment of styles—decorated with turquoises and corals (Amdo).

"The day of the race arrived. Each of the worthiest men had trained his best horse and decked it out in all its finery: thin red cord plaited into its long tail, multicolored ribbons hanging from its mane, a jingling bell at its neck, a finely worked saddle-cloth on its back, the horses looked almost as vain and proud as their owners, as if they too cherished hopes of reigning over Ling....The starting signal was given, they were off. In a flash Gesar's horse overtook all the others. He seemed to fly rather than gallop, his hooves hardly touching the ground. Before his fastest rivals had reached the half-way mark, Gesar passed the finish line, sat on the throne and fixed his calm, confident gaze—clearly that of a divine leader—on the dumbstruck crowd."[1] So goes the tale sung by a Khampa minstrel and heard by Alexandra David-Néel. It is the story of a wild, impulsive boy born in a village in Kham, who conquers the kingdom of Ling. King Gesar, protagonist of this celebrated Tibetan epic, is ruler of the entire universe; endowed with supernatural powers he is able to be present in several places at once and to create ghost caravans complete with tents, servants, lamas and hundreds of

The Sons of Gesar of Ling

horses. In battle, this great hero creates armies of spectral warriors who, at the side of those of flesh and blood, fight and kill their enemies and subjugate demons and rulers of countries at the four corners of the Earth.

Wars and brigandage play a major role in the history of the mountain peoples of Kham—suits of armor were introduced into Tibet from this very region. The earliest known history of Kham dates back to the seventh century AD, when the region became part of the kingdom of Songsten Gampo, a Tibetan king who, in 630 AD, set out on horseback to unify the savage tribes of Central Asia.

As in the past, the Khampa wear brocade robes, trimmed with snow-leopard
or tiger fur, and ornate jewelry at festivals and gatherings. On the previous
pages: left, Alexandra David-Néel pictured with Khampa nomads; right, a
young man shows off his traditional finery (Xinlong; Nyarong, Kham).

Finding allies among the "natural-born" warriors of Kham, Songsten Gampo eventually commanded a huge army, which he used to extend his kingdom throughout Central Asia. He even threatened the Emperor of China who, as a conciliatory gesture, granted him his daughter, Princess Wen Cheng, as a bride. Songsten Gampo made an enduring impression on Kham and its population: his countless courageous deeds mean that he is still remembered as a legendary hero. He is also credited with introducing the Buddhist religion and culture into Tibet.

Formidable warriors like their epic hero Gesar, the Khampa put up tremendous resistance whenever outsiders attempted to conquer or subjugate their country. Unable to defeat them, Genghis Khan was forced to come to terms with them; Mao Tse-tung's Red Army succeeded in invading their territory and reaching Lhasa, but, due to guerrilla warfare waged courageously by the Khampa, the Chinese paid a very high price in human lives.

The Khampa never submitted to the authority of Tibet's central government, resenting its demands for taxes. Fierce bandits but also devout Buddhists, they fought desperately to prevent Chinese occupation. Their defence of Chamdo, Zogqen and Litang against Chinese attack saw extraordinary acts of heroism. The siege of Litang lasted sixty-seven days and ended tragically when Chinese planes bombed the monastery where Khampa guerrillas had sought refuge with the entire local population.

For over a decade the guerrillas recklessly ran the gauntlet of the largest army in the world. They also played a major role in the flight of the Dalai Lama who, disguised as one of them, was escorted to India and safety.

For thousands of years, internal struggles over ownership of grazing land provided an outlet for the natural aggressiveness of the Khampa. Their clans came to form a warrior race that was among the most courageous and fearless in Asia. The impenetrable, forbidding mountains of their homeland were an ideal setting for ambushes and discouraged invaders and merchants.

In Alexandra David-Néel words, Kham was a land where brigandage is "sport and chivalry."[2] At that time, in Amdo as well as in Kham, brigandage was still considered a time-honored occupation which men took up to demonstrate their valor, rather than for the spoils. It was the deed in itself, the "joy of conquest," that led them to follow the caravan trails. Their expeditions were not called robbery but were rather described with such euphemisms as "trading," or—more picturesquely—

"gathering medicinal herbs." Alexander David-Néel's writings contain references to a kind of "secret obligatory service in which men of the tribes were forced to participate in "trading" expeditions, decided by a council of chieftains who also presided over distribution of the spoils."[3] Convinced robbers but devoutly religious, the inhabitants of eastern Tibet follow a "moral code" which demands respect for lamas and other members of the Buddhist clergy and for the poor, and casts disgrace not on astute, successful bandits but on anyone incapable of protecting his own belongings.

From time immemorial, the names of the Khampa and Golok tribes have evoked fears and phantoms of the past. Just as the mere mention of "Redskins" sent shudders down the spine of pioneers and settlers in North America's West, so no pilgrim, merchant or explorer who ventured across the Land of Snows

The history of Kham is a centuries-long tale of wars and brigandage.
Unrivaled as horsemen and superb hunters, the Khampa are passionately
fond of weapons, including guns and swords with silver hilts and sheathes
(Xinlong).

At Litang, high on the plateau at an altitude of 4700 m (15,420 ft), Khampa
horsemen perform sang rituals involving propitiatory fumigation with
juniper branches and herbs in honor of deities of the mountains and sky.

could conceal his fear and apprehension on hearing the word *Khampa* or *Golok*. The Golok peoples (Golok means "rebellious") were renowned as wild, ferocious bandits ruled by a legendary queen, believed to be a reincarnated goddess, whose power was handed down from mother to daughter. Neither the authorities in Lhasa nor in Beijing succeeded in subduing the Khampa and Golok tribes, men of huge build and formidable appearance who were the scourge of

empire. In *Il Milione* (the account of his travels) he described the inhabitants of these lands as "wicked hunters and brigands, who see nothing morally wrong with thieving and killing," people who "worship idols and practice all kinds of magic." Dutreuil de Rhins, in 1894, and Louis Liotard, in 1940, lost their lives in ambushes while exploring these territories. According to Heinrich Harrer, "the region where the Khampa pitch their tents is much feared."

merchant caravans traveling along the route from China to Lhasa.

In previous centuries and into the early twentieth century the few Westerners who crossed these parts described them as ferocious bandits and robbers. One of Marco Polo's missions brought him to this region bordering on the Chinese

Like the "Redskins" of the West of North America in the nineteenth century, the Khampa gave material form to the anxieties and fears of wayfarers: they were the enemy that lay in wait. And, like the Native Americans, they knew their territory intimately. Perfectly camouflaged in their natural environment,

"A father cannot stop his son mounting a wild horse and the son cannot stop the horse from throwing him." (Proverb quoted by Aten in, Horseman in the Snow: The Story of Aten, an Old Khampa Warrior, 1979.)

54

they could interpret every mark on the ground; they were masters at imitating the sounds of animals and the wind, and the noises of the forest. Travelers, pilgrims and merchants who crossed the brigands' territory were alert to the slightest suspect shape or sound, in constant fear of attack. "One of the most typical impressions experienced in this land is of being perpetually on your guard. When walking along, you keep looking right and left to make sure there is nothing in sight; as soon as a shape appears on the horizon, you take out your field-glasses: could it be men or zebras? If this closer view proves the shape to be fellow men, you immediately slip cartridges into your weapons."[4]

The appearance of a Khampa is still unmistakable. Alexandra David-Néel compared one of them to a "hidalgo" who, through some misadventure, had turned brigand. "A true hero of fiction: a man of few words, dark, with watchful eyes, thin lips, long, slightly hooked nose, large silver ring hanging from his right ear and a dignified bearing. What blood can be mixed in this Khampa's veins?"[5]

The origins of the Khampa remain something of a mystery. According to some legends, they are descendants of peoples who once dwelled in the "land of the rock-demons." In ancient Chinese texts they are said to descend from Qiang peoples, who once occupied present-day Kham. They are a proud people—they have been called a "race of kings"—with pronounced features, strong coloring, an aquiline nose and large eyes fixed in a haughty, penetrating gaze.

The Khampa have two great loves: guns and horses. For these nomads, guns—so antiquated they may well be mementos of raids of long ago—have always meant deliverance and survival. From early childhood onwards they learn that only the strongest can survive in the climate and natural environment of their homeland—habitat of wild animals. Guns enable them to defend their herds and grazing lands. Impressive horsemen with a special liking for lively horses, ornate saddles and razor-sharp swords, a Khampa may spend a fortune on a high-spirited stallion with fine proportions. A good horse—a Khampa explains—must be able to carry his rider uphill, but a good horseman must be prepared to walk downhill.

When summer comes, the herdsmen of the high grasslands gather together to celebrate Yaji, the festival of "summer pleasures." The meadows are still empty when we arrive at Litang, in the autonomous Tibetan department of Garze, in the province of Sichuan. But in the space of a few days, almost by magic, an encampment of white tents—practically a town—has sprung up on the site. The white of the tents is relieved by their colored trim in yellow, blue and red, and by decorative patterns formed from popular traditional Tibetan symbols, for instance the Jewel which grants every wish, the Lion of the Snows and the Knot of Never-Ending Love.

During the Yaji summer festival at Litang, horsemen put on displays of various skills: picking up kata *(ceremonial scarves) from the ground; shooting with bows or old muskets; and* goser, *in which they have to bend backwards in the saddle until they touch the ground.*

*"The starting signal was given, they were off. In a flash Gesar's horse over-
took all the others. He seemed to fly rather than gallop, his hooves hardly
touching the ground."[1] On the following pages: the proud expression of a
Khampa nomad from Nyarong seems to reflect his people's longstanding
history as warriors.*

Festivities and gatherings are opportunities to wear fine clothes and ornaments: silver and coral, tiger, sable and snow-leopard furs for the horsemen, resplendent harnesses and saddle-cloths for the horses. On the following pages: groups of horsemen and women wait for the races and dancing to commence at the festival in Litang.

Today, as in Alexandra David-Néel's time, the inhabitants of eastern Tibet use light, white cotton tents at temporary summer campsites and festive gatherings; they are decorated with the Tibetan symbols of good fortune and prosperity (Zogqen, Hor).

After dark, when oil lamps burn in the tents, the shadows of the Khampa projected on the white walls make the plain look like a town populated by ghosts. At first light, smoke begins to rise from the campsite as tea is put on to boil; everyone rises and gets into clothes kept for special occasions: flowing tunics made of fine silk in bright colors symbolizing air (blue), fire (red), earth (yellow) and water (green), trimmed with snow-leopard or tiger fur. The men's hair is tied up with a red woollen band decorated with ivory, silver and coral, wrapped around their head; they wear a huge gold-and-coral earring in their left ear and a sword in their belt: the horsemen of Kham—true heirs of Gesar of Ling—are ready to compete.

Around their neck hangs a *gao*, a reliquary pendant in engraved silver studded with turquoises and corals, which holds an image of a god or a lama. According to Alexandra David-Néel, these horse races originated from the "curious" belief of the peoples of eastern Tibet that, because such events amuse the tutelary gods, they ensure good weather at harvest time.

Before the contest starts, the horsemen walk clockwise three times around a brazier on which juniper branches are burning, holding their frisky stallions by the reins. The gods thus appeased, the competition can begin. A wave of anticipation and excitement sweeps across the plain. All eyes are on the horsemen, who spur their horses into a wild race which has no rules but speed. The horde of men and animals fly along the track, several kilometers long, encouraged by the crowd waiting at the finishing line to cheer the fastest rider.

Next come trials of equestrian skills. The horsemen—alone or in groups—perform acrobatic feats on incredibly fast ponies. Practically born in the saddle, the Khampa are exceptional horsemen. From a horse at the gallop they pick up white ceremonial *kata* scarves, usually exchanged as a sign of respect (on this occasion they conceal a packet of cigarettes, the prize for the successful contestant). They also mount and dismount galloping horses. In an exercise called *goser*, they grip the horse with their thighs only and bend over backwards—as the animal races along at full speed—until their hands touch the ground.

During the week-long festival, the plain at Litang is transformed into a city of tents: the women prepare all sorts of food to offer to family and guests, washed down by chang *(beer brewed from barley). On the following pages: Khampa girls in the vicinity of the campsite, wearing fine brocade dresses and* poden, *decorated with large silver studs called* borchen.

To perform the ancient folk dances of Nyarong, these men—pictured in Xinlong—wear white robes with long sleeves, symbolizing affluence and abundance.

Amber, the color of earth, and coral, symbolizing light, interweaved in the hair of these young Khampa girls are a sign that they are of marriageable age (Xinlong).

In another competition, firmly seated on decorative saddle-cloths, they raise their bow and arrow or an old rifle and—sometimes from beneath the horse's belly—aim at minute targets stuck into a clod of earth. The contest is hard and more than once a horseman finds himself on the ground, among the sympathetic cries of shame from the crowd.

Our senses are dazed by roars from the spectators, shouts of contestants and the deafening thud of hooves. All we can see are the colored figures flashing past us, seemingly carried by the wind, ghosts of one-time brigands and warriors heading into forays or battles. Between races contestants make their colorfully adorned mounts rear and prance, in further displays of bravado designed to draw admiring glances from the women.

The women stroll back and forth, decked out in beautiful brocade dresses trimmed with sable. They wear traditional jewelry, heavy with silver, coral and amber, and the *poden* headdress, comprised of one or more waist-length strips of black fabric, attached to which are pieces of amber, coral or large silver studs, called *borchen*. Other silver or gold studs are fixed to the *charma*, a fine silk belt from which hang silver chains, long rows of coral beads or pieces of jewelry like the *losar*, an engraved silver medallion held in place by a large half-moon shaped brooch. Some of them—authentic nomads, a lama tells us—wear their hair in tiny braids and a *poden* with large pieces of amber surmounted by coral.

Among the beads of the necklaces worn by this young Khampa girl are zi, *highly valued, semiprecious stones with black veining. The young man opposite is dressed in his costume for a performance based on the legendary tale of Gesar of Ling (Xinlong).*

The women "…wear their hair gathered in tens of tiny braids, decorated with big silver or even gold studs. Their dresses are highly colorful, in bright reds and gaudy greens."[6]

Nomads think every woman should be dressed this way when she marries, to show she is the daughter of "loving parents." When the races are over, men and women form a circle to dance the *dro*, a traditional Tibetan folk song and dance; as they chant, they move with slow, graceful steps, bending forward and making the long sleeves of their dresses twirl and flutter.

A festive mood fills the air as crowds throng traders' stalls, areas set aside for dancing and performances, and eating

amulets; or simply to meet friends, arrange marriages or ask questions of lamas beneath the huge monastery tent.

As night approaches, lamps are lit and the inhabitants of this "town" once more appear as shadows. It is a spectacular and moving sight. The stresses and strains of our life in the West are forgotten; the event we have been privileged to witness, has enabled us — like Alexandra David-Néel — to "get out of our skin", "experience a myriad of new sensations" and understand "how much fantasy and

places where beer flows in abundance. For people who live scattered over such an immense region, the festival of summer pleasures is a vital opportunity to barter goods and do business. It may be a chance to find a good horse, a saddle, boots, silk fabric, medicinal plants and

poetry can be contained in a greasy sheepskin robe, sitting close to a raging fire of yak dung and holding a bowl of buttered tea, while the simple folk of the caravan, gathered around a fire nearby, sing about the adventures of Gesar, conqueror of the Land of Hor."[7]

"*L ha gyalo! Dé Tamtché pham!*...The gods have won, the demons are defeated!"[1] A shout of triumph which—like every Tibetan—Alexandra David-Néel and the lama Yongden (her inseparable traveling companion and adopted son) sent echoing around them whenever, on their travels, they reached the top of a pass or mountain. It was followed by an auspicious phrase used by Buddhists—"may all beings be happy"—pronounced facing the four quarters, the zenith and the nadir. Passes and hilltops in the Land of Snows are littered with huge piles of stones called *latsè*: rustic altars on which monks, lamas, pilgrims and wayfarers place stones, completing the ritual with shouts of victory and praise to the mountain-gods. Fluttering from these piles of stones are *rlung-ta*, "horses of the wind:" cotton prayer flags in the five colors symbolizing air, clouds, fire, earth and water, with sacred formulae and the "horse of the wind" painted on them. This mythical creature carries on its back the jewel that grants all desires and symbolically conveys the prayers written on each flag across valleys and mountains, riding on the wind.

Horses of the Wind

"Horses of the wind" are one of the many manifestations of faith found scattered across the Land of Snows. For centuries, monks and pilgrims have left tangible signs of their devotion, for instance *mani* prayer-walls, made from stones carved or engraved with sacred images or mantras. To celebrate the month of the bull, nomads erect light, pagoda-shaped structures made of cotton sheets, called *targö*, printed with mantras, to which are fastened tongues of material colored blue, white, yellow, red and green.

Elsewhere, singly or in rows, are found *chörten*: the square base of these Lamaist shrines symbolizes the Earth, the dome Water, the conical spire Fire, the canopy Air, and the sun and moon placed on the top the Heavens—all symbols of the Wisdom of Buddha. Prayer-wheels are large brass, copper or wooden cylinders on which mantras are engraved; when moved by wind, water or the hands of worshippers they send thousands of prayers heavenwards.

pation of its inhabitants" (in *Le Tibet revolté*, 1912).

According to Alexandra David-Néel Buddhist monks "do more traveling in Tibet than traders."[2] They journey over plateaux and through valleys on horseback, on foot and nowadays, when possible, in trucks, to beg for alms for their monastery, to recite prayers and read the Book of the Dead or, as in the past, to search for a spiritual teacher or holy scriptures.

Strange-shaped rocks are believed to be the work of the gods or an apparition of a deity. In any journey across eastern Tibet, mysticism and the supernatural are ever present; Jacques Bacot described these territories as a land of "herdsmen and monks, forbidden to foreigners, isolated from the world and so close to the heavens that prayer is the natural occu-

Traveling alone or in groups, pilgrims use any means of transport to visit monasteries and shrines across the country, some famous, others little known. Retracing the steps of many thousands who have gone before them, they circumambulate monasteries, *chörten*, *latsè* or sacred mountains. These circuits are an essential part of their rites of worship and

Rows of prayer-wheels in the monastery at Kumbum (opposite) and along the outside wall of the monastery of Labrang (above), built in 1709 by Ngawang Tsondu. On the previous pages: left, Madame Alexandra David-Néel with her lama companion, Yongden; right, a lama rapt in prayer holds a trenua *— a rosary made up of 108 beads (Zogqen).*

prayer. Pilgrims recite prayers as they walk round: clockwise for Buddhists, anti-clockwise for worshippers of the pre-Buddhist religion, *Bön-po*. Even illiterate Tibetans know by heart devotional phrases like *Om Mani Padme Hum*, the mantra of Avalokitesvara (Bodhisattva, symbol of universal compassion, spiritual leader of Tibet, of whom the Dalai Lamas, rulers of Tibet, are believed to be reincarnations), or *Om a Hum Vajra Guru Padma Siddhi Hum*, which is the mantra of Padmasambhava, the "lotus born" Tantric teacher, whom Tibetans call Guru Rinpoche. Though devout, few Amdowa and Khampa know the profound meaning of the mantras they recite.

As they circumambulate the sacred place, some hold prayer-wheels containing fragments of holy scriptures on paper or cloth; others run rosaries of 108 beads through their fingers. The most devout prostrate themselves at each step, arms outstretched, hands joined, forehead touching the ground. On one of our visits to Lhagong, a monastery destroyed in the Cultural Revolution and since rebuilt, we came across some pilgrims doing precisely this as they circled the monastery. On one side this monastery overlooks the main road to Lhasa. Each time a truck passed by—and there was a steady flow of traffic—a dense cloud of dirty-white dust descended on the prostrated bodies of the pilgrims, covering them with a thick layer. An old Khampa woman observed the scene as she sat turning her prayer-wheel in her hand. She told us that, although fewer than in the olden days, there are still pilgrims who go the whole way to Lhasa prostrating themselves at each step, oblivious of the traffic and indifferent to the danger.

Pilgrimage is a means of acquiring merits and increasing *karma*, and thus – after a round of rebirths and deaths – a person may achieve Enlightenment. The difficulties and dangers of the journey do not discourage pilgrims, in fact they increase the value of the penance. They may do endless circuits of holy mountains like Mount Kailas – one circuit can cancel the sins of this life, ten circuits the sins of all lives, while a hundred circuits confers the state of Buddha in this life. There are many perils on the way: extreme cold, lack of food and shelter, hailstorms, blizzards and, in the past, attacks by brigands. The country is unpitying: almost impenetrable paths run alongside sheer precipices, fast-flowing rivers rush under precarious suspended bridges, avalanches come hurtling down mountainsides, forests harbor many hidden dangers.

A lama pictured at the monastery of Lhagong, north of Kangding, the ancient Tachienlu, rebuilt since the Cultural Revolution.

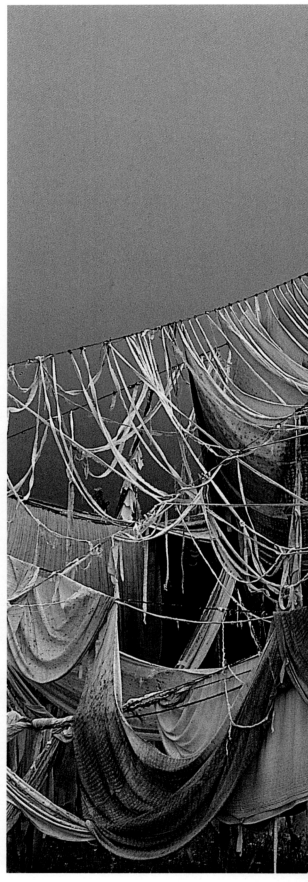

Nomads and pilgrims construct light, pagoda-shaped structures with targö—cotton sheets printed with sacred formulae, on to which are fastened tongues of blue, white, yellow, green and red material. (Plains east of Anye Machin, Amdo.)

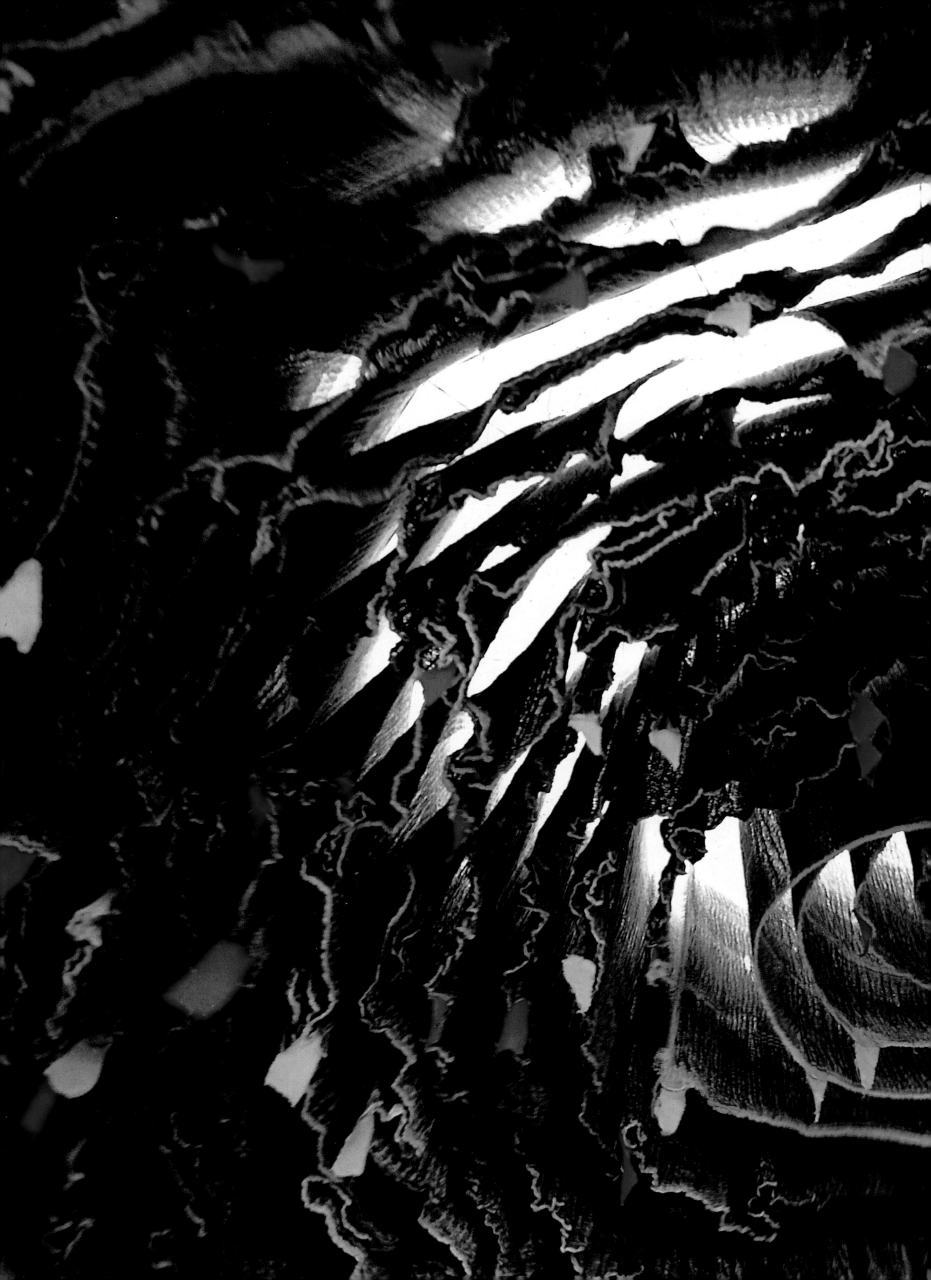

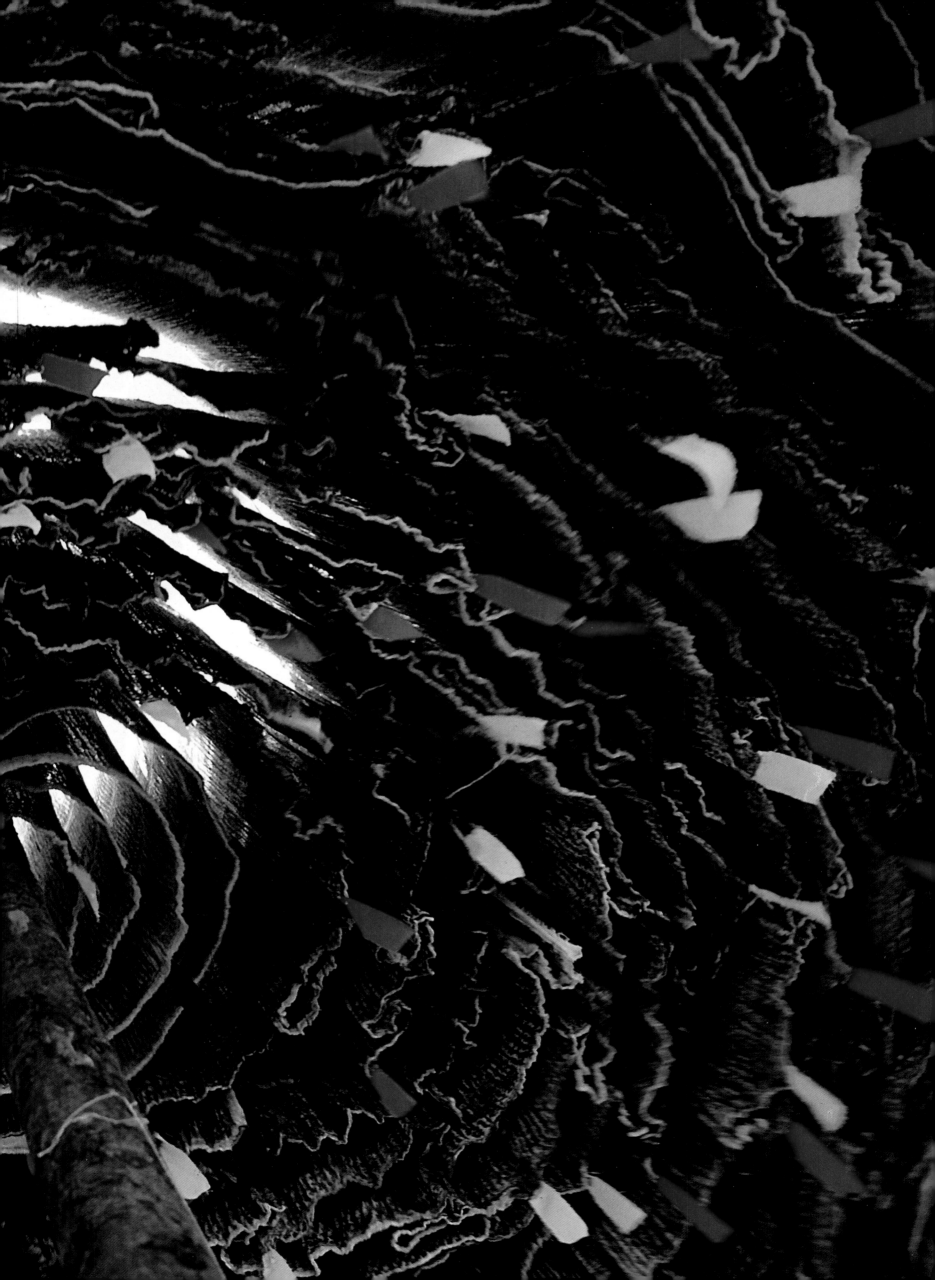

In a wintry landscape in the plains of Tanggor, in Amdo, along the Gar Qu, a tributary of the Yellow River, a row of chörten *marks the path followed by pilgrims performing ritual circumambulations.*

In the imaginations of travelers, fear has created a world of spirits and demons. Alexandra David-Néel tells of beliefs born of these fears, such as "a demon-tree which grows on the edge of cliffs, grabs wayfarers with its thorny branches and drags them into the abyss"[3] or evil spirits which wander across steppes and through forests in search of men and creatures from whom to snatch the "breath of life." In the far western regions of China people lived a solitary existence in a wilderness where they were constantly prey to the forces of nature. It is easy to understand how the cult of natural deities, like mountain-gods and lake-gods, developed among these peoples and how their belief in spirits and divinities hiding in springs and rocks, in the depths of rivers and lakes, or on nearby mountains became an intrinsic part of their everyday life.

These beliefs were the legacy of the original local cults and of the *Bön-po* religion, practiced before the introduction of Buddhism. Traces of animistic rites exist in present-day Tibet, especially in Kham. In a natural setting so densely populated with spirits, *Bön-po* priests enjoyed great esteem. They had magical powers and were credited with the ability to converse with demons and phantoms and control their actions.

Buddhist doctrines were introduced into Tibet by Padmasambhava, the powerful Indian sage who came to the country in 755 AD at the invitation of Thi-srong-detsan (a successor of Songsten Gampo). This teacher and mystic realized he would never succeed in eradicating the beliefs and superstitions firmly rooted in the grassland deserts. But he demonstrated that his own magical art was more potent than that of the *Bön-po* priests and, having won the trust of the people, he incorporated certain aspects

Prayer-wheels, carved or incised with mantra, are turned in the hands of
pilgrims, sending thousands of prayers to heaven (Labrang). Opposite, an
old Khampa woman visits the monastery of Lhagong. On the following
pages: nomads turn the huge prayer-wheel at Waqen, in Amdo.

of the *Bön-po* religion into Buddhist practices. Buddhism became the national religion two centuries later, under the influence of great Tantric teachers from India and their Tibetan disciples. Many different sects developed: one was versed in the methods of the "Short Path," by which its members could attain Supreme Liberation, or Nirvana, in the course of a single existence. As well as sects formed by followers of Milarepa, Padmasambhava and other teachers, known as Red Caps, in the early fifteenth century a new order was formed: these were the Gelugpa or Yellow Hat sect, founded by Tsongkapa, a native of Amdo, who was the first Dalai Lama. An influential clerical organization was thus established, which often held temporal as well as spiritual powers. Monasteries were the cultural centers of Tibet and

it became the only country to adopt a succession through reincarnation, with power passed on through the *tulku* (reincarnations of important lamas).

Over the centuries temporal authority changed hands due to internal struggles and foreign wars, but the spiritual influence of Lamaism (the Tibetan form of Buddhism) spread to the courts of the Mongol and Chinese emperors. Monks and pilgrims made an important contribution to the dissemination of Tibetan culture, extending the borders of a huge imaginary country united by Buddhism.

Although the Land of the Gentlemen Brigands lies outside the geographical boundaries of Tibet, its "horses of the wind" and its *latsè* are unmistakable signs of this influence, which endures in spite of the Cultural Revolution and the exile of the Dalai Lama.

"Beneath a low, grey, snow-laden sky, against the backdrop of a completely white mountain, a herd of yaks moves slowly forward; their huge black bodies stand out against the snow, its whiteness eventually merging with the heavy, leaden gray of the sky: a symphony in black and white, reminiscent of an etching. But what artist could ever render the real tones of such a picture? These are things which dazzle, bewitch and captivate. There is nothing to equal the light of Tibet and the fascinating effect it has on things."[1] It is early morning on a bitterly cold January day in the Land of the Gentlemen Brigands and our faces are stung by a ferocious wind blowing across the plateau, which is only slightly dusted with snow. Our horses have still not shaken off the freezing cold of the night and seem a little unsteady as they move forward. They occasionally drop their heads to pull a few blades of yellow grass from the snow. Winter has turned the plateau and the valleys into a fairy-tale snowscape. Nature has been imprisoned by the freezing cold. Thundering waterfalls have been silenced and are now ice sculptures, suspended in mid-air; branches of shrubs are

Winter in the Land of Snows

dazzling icicles; the mist which rises from the plains has left the trees frostbound, transforming the woods into enchanted forests. Wanden—a *dokpa* who spends the whole year on the plateau—has agreed to accompany us to the site where his family is camped for the winter. Wrapped in a *lokbar*—the heavy sheepskin robe which nomads wear wool-side next to their naked skin, even in winter—he enters a long, narrow valley protected by two rows of hills, their tops disappearing into the low sky, heavy with its menace of snow. We hear the muffled echo of the cries of herdsmen calling to their yaks, but there is no sign of either men or animals.

A small train of men and women on huge yaks used as pack animals are soon visible, coming towards us from the far end of the valley. Emerging from a young woman's sheepskin dress is the head of a small child, fast asleep against his mother's back and rocked to and fro with each step of the yak.

Winter does not prevent the pastoral nomads of the plateau from continuing their daily lives, constantly taking their animals to pasture. Watching over them is Dolma, Tibetan personification of Tara, the Hindu goddess of energy, very popular among Lamaists. As the protectress of wayfarers, Dolma is addressed by reciting a long formula to appeal for help. Alexandra David-Néel explained how this also serves to "render invisible to brigands any traveler who recites the formula with faith and has a pure heart. The tale is told of some traders at the head of a long caravan who in this way succeeded in passing unnoticed through bands of brigands. Or even more remarkably, instead of traders or pilgrims, the evildoers saw a procession of goddesses pass by."[2]

In every part of the world there are legends and epic poems that tell of amazing feats performed thanks to the gift of invisibility. Alexandra David-Néel relates that Tibetans believe in a *dipching*, "the wood that hides," a talisman that makes anyone holding it invisible (some say it is a special piece of wood which crows can recognize; others that it is a feather of a crow or magpie).

On reaching the river, Wanden dismounts and, making his way along the bank with his thick felt-and-leather boots, he looks carefully at its frozen surface. The ice and the water beneath conceal countless perils but Wanden is familiar with the route to the winter pasturelands and knows exactly where it is possible to ford the river. After knotting his horse's tail, he gets back in the saddle and ventures on to the frozen surface, testing the ice. His horse slips and slides. Wanden urges him on, then makes him rear up until the ice gives way and he sinks into the water, up to his belly. When they emerge on the opposite bank, the horse looks like some mythical creature: half animal, half ice.

"…immense waterfalls turned to sparkling ice hang suspended from the
tops of the rocks; a blindingly white, awe-inspiring world above the dark
line of the pine trees…"[3] On the previous pages: left, Madame Alexandra
David-Néel during a moment of rest; right, an Amdowa herdsman copes
with the harsh reality of winter. On the following pages: the forests of
Erlang Shan caught in an icy grip.

"Rocks and branches outlined shapes of fantastic figures…invisible beings seemed to surround us."[4] On the following pages: a layer of snow covers winter grazing lands on the slopes of Anye Machin, in Amdo.

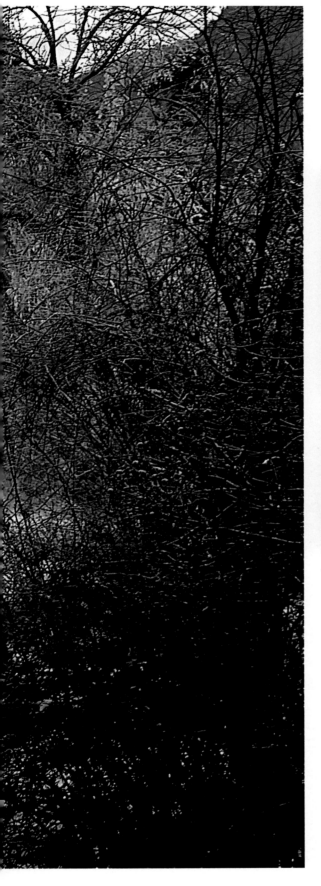

Wintering at an altitude of 4000 m (13,000 ft) is not for the feeble or faint-hearted; only the real *dokpa* know how to survive. As autumn comes to an end the herds are driven to winter pastures on the lower slopes of the mountains, in sunny valleys protected from gales and blizzards. Winter pasturelands are vitally important. No herds are allowed to graze there in summer and autumn; the herdsmen legally entitled to occupy that land might otherwise see their animals die of hunger in winter for lack of food. While summer camps are moved fairly frequently in search of better grazing land, winter camps are permanent. To protect animals and tents from wind, snowstorms and hungry wolves, the *dokpa* build enclosures of head-high walls using clods of mud mixed with dung. This same material is sometimes used to construct humble, single-room dwellings which they can live in during the coldest months and abandon when winter is over. From afar, these simple, low, mud buildings—hidden behind the protective walls from which prayer flags flutter in the wind—look like miniature citadels, built to withstand an invisible enemy.

Wanden's family is camped close to a torrent, from which the women can easily get water by breaking the surface ice where it is thinnest. Since they have no stores of fodder on which to feed their animals, the nomads have to take their sheep, goats and yaks to pasture every single day of the year. Each morning, after milking, herdsmen on horseback drive the animals to the lower slopes of hills or to wide valleys which the chilling wind has swept clear of snow.

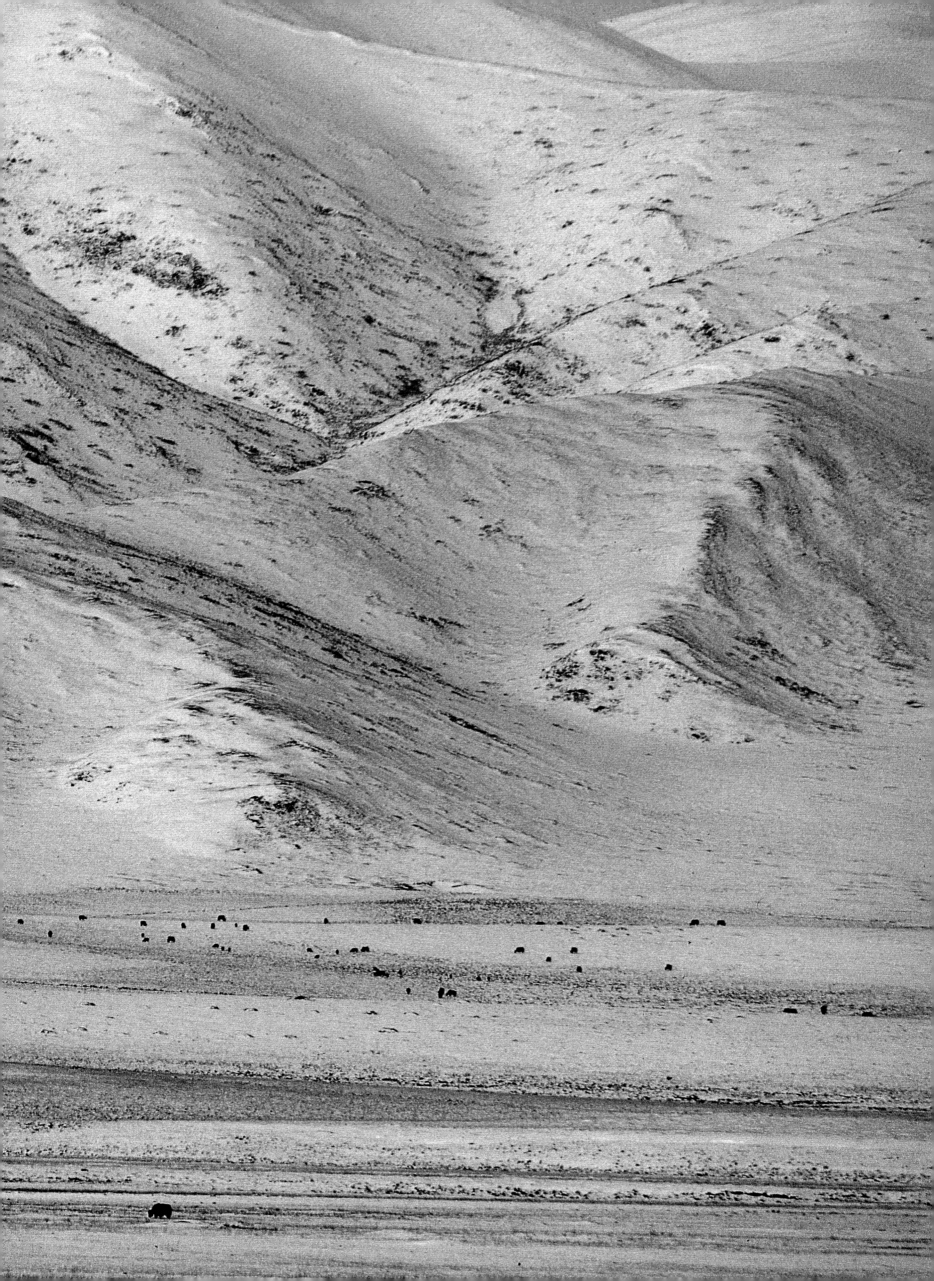

Their faces ruddy-red under their fox-fur hats, the nomads spend the whole day following their herds. As evening approaches, they take them to drink at torrents where the fast flow of the water prevents the entire surface from turning to ice. At dusk, when the *dokpa* return to the campsite, their faces are sometimes so stiff with cold they are unable to speak. But they take the rigors of this severe climate for granted, being indifferent to ice, snow and bitter cold. Nomads accept winter as an inevitability which does not stop them going about their daily business. Their livestock is their most precious resource and they continue to milk their herds and flocks and take them to graze, irrespective of the weather. But during winter only the men and most experienced boys take the animals to pasture. As Wanden explains to us, this season is the most difficult for pastoral nomads. Sheep and goats may give birth when there is still snow on the ground and temperatures are very low. A herdsman must stay very close to the mother, ready to intervene straight after the birth by drying and covering the newly born lamb or kid, which might otherwise freeze to death. For this reason herdsmen never lose sight of pregnant ewes and take pains to ensure newborn animals are kept warm, in saddlebags carried by yaks or horses, or even in the front pocket of their own *lokbar*.

In winter, wolves are the nomads' greatest enemy. Hunger drives these predators close to campsites and houses, sometimes in broad daylight. The herdsmen have few means of defense: enclosures made of mud and dung or sheets of cloth, sticks, antiquated rifles and dogs. Often even the ferocious mastiffs cannot prevent animals from being attacked. Wanden's brother proudly shows us a wolfskin hanging outside his tent. For a week—he tells us—the wolf attacked his own sheep and the flock of other nomads camped not far distant. But one day, after it attacked one of his sheep in broad daylight, he at last managed to kill it. He takes great pleasure in displaying his long-barrelled shotgun and a support, fashioned out of antelope horns, used to rest the weapon on the ground and take aim. It used to be the tradition for a nomad who killed a wolf to skin it and then go around the camp with the skin, "begging:" the community was expected to make an offering to the person who had freed them from the danger.

Hunting animals for their fur is against the law but selling pelts is a valuable source of income for the nomads. In spite of the law, and Buddhist principles, such opportunities are often difficult to turn down. Fox pelts are used to make warm hats for the winter and sable or snow-leopard fur trim the robes worn by both men and women during festivities. The old *dokpa* disapprove of killing animals solely for their skins. One of them explains to us that it might make the mountain angry and it could show its displeasure by taking away the life of the hunter or one of his family.

A woman drives a small herd of yaks towards the plains of Hongyuan, in
Amdo. Even in winter the inhabitants of the uplands continue their
nomadic life, constantly looking for grazing.

In winter, camp is often pitched near rivers flowing fast enough to prevent the build up of thick ice, so the nomads have a source of water (River Xiqu, Kham).

"That morning, a bright sun lit up the blue sky and brought a glow to the yellow earth, after the frost and ice of winter."[5] (River Gar Qu, Amdo.)

Nomads slaughter animals at the beginning of winter. After grazing all through summer and autumn, the beasts have accumulated fat and have not yet started to lose weight; the cold, dry winter climate freezes the carcasses and makes it possible to store the meat well into spring. The best parts are cut into narrow strips and then dried in the tent, on the male side.

For herdsmen, their flocks and herds represent their capital assets, which they try to keep intact and increase; they therefore sell or slaughter only the number of animals they think can be replaced by newborn animals. In addition, they also slaughter only as many animals as are necessary to provide enough meat for their needs.

It is left to the most experienced men to decide which animals are to be slaughtered. Most Tibetan herdsmen do not kill their animals themselves: as Buddhists they believe this could mean a bad *karma* so, whenever possible, they leave the actual slaughter to other Tibetans or to Chinese, who are paid to do the job.

Wanden walks over to a huge yak used as a pack animal, which is tied up close to the tent. This beast, which has a red wool bow in its ear, will never be slaughtered. It is a *tsethar*, the name given by the nomadic herdsmen to animals which have received immunity from slaughter according to a custom originating in the belief that the life of the owner will thus also be prolonged. Nomads believe that the rituals which free the sheep or yak from being killed also avert the death of the herdsman by eliminating dangerous events that are a threat to him. Once the creature has been redeemed from being killed by the mantras recited by a lama, it may not be slaughtered and is fed and cared for until it dies a natural death. Its horns, incised with mantras, will then be

"The herds live outside all year round. As winter approaches they are driven to places which catch the sun, in valleys shielded from the wind."[6]
Opposite, Amdowa children in front of enclosures built of mud and dung to
shelter animals and tents from the wind.

A group of nomads crosses the vast deserts of grass in search of the best place to pitch camp for the winter. Dokpa wear fox-fur hats to protect them from the intense cold (near Roergai, Amdo).

placed on a *mani* wall or on a *latsè* and will guarantee the favored animal a better reincarnation.

Two nomads from a neighboring hill call in at Wanden's campsite, riding on horseback. They are on their way to Hongyuan, a town on the plateau about a day's ride away, where they hope to sell a yak pelt. The proceeds will be used to buy barley to make *tsampa*, bricks of compressed tea, dried fruit, rice and utensils.

themselves in the few smoky eating places, where they drink buttered tea and the local spirits.

The *dokpa* rarely return to their camps without challenging someone to a spirited game of billiards, played on large tables set up out of doors. At this time of year the game is not always finished. The weather can change amazingly quickly: snow-laden clouds carried by gusting winds mean that a dry, sunny day can end with blizzards.

In winter, when traveling is slower and more difficult due to the harsh conditions, excursions into town to trade goods are also an opportunity to see different people and exchange news. The *dokpa* linger in the stores and warm

The billiard tables are hurriedly covered up again with nylon sheeting and the *dokpa*—their horses or yaks laden with provisions—start back towards the mountains, ready to return to their camps and the wintry solitude.

In winter, trips to the little town of Hongyuan, in Amdo, are made for both business and pleasure. On the following pages: wrapped in their heavy winter lokbar, two dokpa journey back towards their mountain campsite.

In the very beginning—so the legend goes—Avalokitesvara (in Tibetan Chenrezi), the Bodhisattva of compassion, made incarnate on Earth as a monkey, was moved to pity by the lamentations of a rock-demon tormented by solitude, and married her. Six children were born to them—half human, half monkey—forefathers of the six tribes of Tibet today. To his children Avalokitesvara allocated the forests of the South, but they and their offspring suffered from the summer heat and winter cold and very soon had nothing to eat. Avalokitesvara felt sorry for them and provided them with six different seeds: barley, corn, sesame, rice, pea and mustard. The first cultivated fields thus appeared in the valley of the Yarlung; the monkeys became men and spread throughout Tibet. The legend points to the important role of agriculture in a country where most of the inhabitable land is given over to pasturage. The nomadic herdsmen of the plateau and the agricultural peasants of the valleys have always been interdependent. According to Sir Aurel Stein (an archaeologist renowned for his travels in Central Asia), the environment itself imposes a dual

In the Valleys of the Gyarongpas

morphology on Tibetan life. On one hand there is a single group—people of the valleys—whose life follows the seasons: farmers in winter, herdsmen on mountain pastures in summer. On the other, are two groups—nomads and sedentary agriculturalists—who live in symbiosis. Because the produce of farming and pasturage was bartered, trade links became established between the world of the *dokpa*, high on the plateau, and the land of the Gyarongpas (meaning "people of the Chinese valleys"). According to Alexandra David-Néel, the Gyarongpas were populations of Tibetan origin who settled in the Chinese (*gya*) valleys (*rong*) many centuries ago.

Since time immemorial, a part of the population of Kham and Amdo has lived a semi-nomadic existence. Summers are spent on the move, winters in houses built of stone on the valley slopes.

Aurel Stein tells how, as long ago as 1769, the clerics of Kham went begging in the pastures in summer and in the cultivated valleys in autumn and winter, and how, in the nineteenth century, chiefs from the Lang clan, which originated in the valleys of Kham, used to say: "When we go to the pastures (*brog*) in summer, we find good grass; when we go to the village (*yul*) in autumn, we find good soil."

Alexandra David-Néel described the *rongdok* as people who "for part of the year live in small hamlets and cultivate their land; then, in summer, some of them—often the women—are left to guard their simple dwellings and to gather in and store the harvest. Everyone else leaves, with the herds, to live on grazing land in the mountains."[1]

This lifestyle has survived the attempts made by the Chinese in the 1960s to force the nomads to settle in one place, by introducing agrarian reform and pastoral communes. After political leadership in China changed hands, the communes were abolished and most of the nomads resumed their previous transhuman ways. However, the close interdependence which bound the inhabitants of the plateau and the peoples of the valleys was seriously weakened.

Previous pages: left, Madame Alexandra David-Néel is accompanied along a trail in Kham; right, mist envelops the forests of Daxue Shan. Illustrated on these and following pages are two villages along the Dajin Chuan river, linked at the bottom of the valley by precarious-looking wooden bridges.

Known as the "Land of the Four Rivers" (Salween, Mekong, Yangtze, Yarlung), eastern Tibet is hard hit by the monsoon in summer. Only the sturdiest bridges withstand the rushing torrents as rivers and streams flood the valleys.

In the Valleys of the Gyarongpas

Many roads have now been opened, convoys of trucks have replaced caravans and all kinds of goods from the cities and plains of China reach the plateau. But the territories where the nomads live, moving from one grazing area to another are immense, and often many days' trek from a main road. The nomads therefore continue to maintain their centuries-old customs, although in their tents, together with churns and shotguns, a place has now been found for colored thermos, flasks and household wares of Chinese manufacture.

In the valleys, always places of passage where Tibetan and Chinese cultures met, the Chinese presense is more marked. Officials and policemen are Chinese, as are merchants and owners of eating places; they control trade and business generally. The Tibetans themselves are mostly farmers. In many valleys they still live the semi-nomadic life of pasturage in summer and cultivation during the rest of the year.

Each year, at the time of the first new moon, the fields are prepared for ploughing by the women and children, who gather up stones and spread manure. The men walk behind the *dzo*— a hybrid obtained by crossing a bull with a *dri*—which pulls a wooden or iron plough. Peasants take great care of these beasts since they believe the prosperity of their family depends on their strength. In farming communities of the more remote valleys, the cycle of cultivation, as in the past, is accompanied by rituals of propitiation, such as fumigations dedicated to the spirits of the fields, or the consultation of almanacs or a lama experienced in Tantric practices to establish the most favorable time for harvest.

In the deep valleys where the plateau drops down towards China, villages are often perched on mountain slopes, facing towards the sun, below forests of pine trees. Constructed of stones laid without mortar or of clay, the houses look like miniature fortresses. Although close to other neighboring dwellings, each one is completely separate and has a boundary wall (its height an indication of the wealth of its owner); this surrounds the courtyard where pack animals (yaks and *dzo*) used for caravan expeditions were once kept.

As Alexandra David-Néel reported, the direction a house faced was considered very important in Tibet: even today, lamas and oracles are consulted to establish a propitious site and to consecrate the ground on which the building is to stand. The houses have three or four floors: animals are kept on the windowless ground floor, together with farming and shearing tools. In some tribes, like the Sharwa of Amdo, women once gave birth on the ground floor, considered the least pure place, closer to the earth- and water-spirits which watch over the prosperity of the house and its occupants. The middle floors form the living area, reached up a staircase made from a huge tree trunk, in which are carved thirteen steps (thirteen is considered a lucky

A horse loaded with merchandise, not far from Rilou, is a reminder of the time when "trading" was a quaint euphemism used to refer to forays made by brigands. Opposite, inhabitants of the valleys, dressed in their finest clothes for a wedding (Kham).

number). Leaning at an almost vertical angle and leading up to a trapdoor, the trunk ladder can be removed to prevent access to the upper floors, thus affording greater protection.

A large terrace (or flat roof), often facing south, overlooks the courtyard and valley. Here, in winter, people warm themselves in the sun, children play and women card, spin and weave, or thresh cereals. At the topmost point of the house is the shrine. Here, amid butter lamps, are images of the Dalai Lama, Buddha and Padmasambhava, as well as silver or copper bowls full of water. Widely used as an offering in Tibet, water symbolizes the equality of worshippers, irrespective of position and wealth.

Social and family life center on the room which houses the fireplace; it usually has no windows other than the *kung*, the square opening made in the ceiling to let out the smoke from the fire. As in the nomads' tents, the fireplace separates the women's area from that reserved for the men, which is situated towards the outside. An old Khampa woman tells us of a tradition which states that it bodes ill for a family's womenfolk if a man spends too long in their area.

Even today, access to the region where the Gyarongpas live is extremely difficult at any time of year. The mountain systems of eastern Tibet are among the most unruly on earth. Cutting across the boundless grasslands of the plateau are deep valleys which form innumerable

furrows, rapidly descending in elevation in the direction of China. Through these valleys flow the most important rivers of eastern Asia: the Salween, the Mekong, the Yangtze with its tributary the Yarlung, and the Huang He, or Yellow River.

Almost impassable roads and steep paths wind their way up and down the slopes of hills and valleys. The once thick and luxuriant forests (now decimated by deforestation) are still home to wolves, bears and the increasingly rare snow-leopard. Here, summer is the monsoon season. The mountain peaks disappear as dense mist creeps down through the valleys and forests. Rivers and streams swell into rushing floods which obliterate roads and paths and carry away frail bridges, leaving entire villages isolated for days.

In 1933 Alexandra David-Néel described her experiences and offered guidance: "My sincere advice to any travelers tempted to journey through the far west regions of China in spring or summer is to refrain from doing so. This is the season of the rains and…I have on many occasions experienced the problems this causes: roads swept away by landslides, valleys awash with flood water, collapsed bridges, cascading water suddenly pouring down on sleeping travelers from a damaged roof, mud and damp that increase the dirtiness of native dwellings. A pilgrim's enthusiasm is severely tested."[2]

Opposite, a young bride awaits the arrival of the groom. Above, stones engraved with sacred formulae are set beneath a decorated window (Rinzhubtang, Kham).

"Among these innocent-looking fields and pastures tales of brigands and
murdered wayfarers are no longer frightening, even if they are all too true,
the peasants of the region combine their peaceful work as agriculturalists
with the more fiery activities of brigands."[3]

The **rongdok** *"for part of the year cultivate their land…then, in summer, some of them—often the women—are left to guard their simple dwellings and to gather in and store the harvest."*[1] (Near Dangba.)

1922: Alexandra David-Néel wrote to her husband, Philippe: "I saw some wonderful dancing.... The dancers were possessed by the devil, they whirled and spinned till I felt dizzy."[1] 1992: Katok Gompa. Some two thousand pilgrims crowd in spellbound silence to watch monks perform the "mysteries," sacred ceremonial dances whose origins are attributed to the Buddha Sakyamuni (Gautama), founder of Buddhism. To reach the monastery, nomads and peoples of the valleys have undertaken a long, costly journey, some on horseback, some on yaks, others traveling as far as possible in trucks, packed like sardines, then continuing on foot. They have pitched their white tents in every possible place, even on the roofs of the monks' dwellings. For them, today as seventy years ago, *cham* ritual dances are a religious occasion and also a welcome opportunity to meet up with other inhabitants of isolated parts of this region. There are about four hundred monks at Katok, including many lamas and *tulku* from monasteries as far away as India. From all over the province people have come to watch the sacred dances and prostrate themselves before deities and lamas to

Mysteries of Tibet

receive their blessing. Jostling together, "their bent heads knocking as they push forward like a flock of frightened sheep,"[2] as Alexandra David-Néel described the scene to her husband, they hurry forward to receive the blessing. It is not a symbolic blessing like the Pope's, extended to all those present, but actual physical contact: each head must be touched by the hands of the lama or his *dorje*, the "diamond" or "thunderbolt" sceptre, a Tantric ritual object symbolizing the state of enlightenment. Only in this way can believers benefit from the health-giving energy that emanates from the lama.

The pilgrims form an endless human snake along the path winding up to the monastery. They stand in this queue for hours, oblivious to the wind and dust, waiting for the lamas to pass by so they may touch their robe and receive their blessing: *tse ring rilbou*, "pills of long life," charged with the lama's vital force.

The deep notes of *dung-chen*, the long telescope-shaped horns, announce the imminent commencement of the performance of the dance. Each representing a deity, the actor-monks enter the enclosure of the monastery courtyard. The harmonious movements of the dancers do not seem to be impeded by their huge masks, some still made of wood but most of papier mâché. The attentive audience does not miss a single gesture.

A shudder goes through the crowd as monks wearing masks depicting irate deities appear. These deities represent restless, dynamic workings of the mind and the masks worn by the dancers have large, golden faces framed by five small, white skulls, a ferocious expression and a third eye—the eye of transcendental perception—painted vertically in the center of the forehead.

The beautiful, ornate costumes are made from silk, brocade or cotton in colors taken from Tantric iconography. The entrance of further deities is met with murmurs of admiration: the sacred deer—wearing a brightly colored costume and a mask fashioned in the shape of the head of a deer, with colourful ribbons decorating its horns—is followed by a long line of dancers who impersonate different deities with human bodies

The atsara – opposite, one with his face covered with flour – provide breaks
in the traditional phases of the cham with their comic antics which amuse
the crowds of spectators (Litang, Kham). Previous pages: left, two of these
clowns in a photo by Alexandra David-Néel; right, an atsara performing in
the monastery of Katok, Kham.

Masks depicting angry gods have faces framed by five skulls, with a third eye—the eye of transcendental perception—painted on the forehead (Katok Gompa, Kham).

but with animal heads. The different phases of the *cham* are accompanied by music: the dull, solemn sound of drums (*nga*), silver-decorated shells (*dung-kar*) and *gya-ling*, an instrument which is similar to the oboe.

The first *cham* was reportedly mounted by Padmasambhava at Samye, Tibet's earliest Buddhist monastery, in the eighth century. The ritualistic form of the dance can vary in style and expression, according to where it is performed. Each monastery has its own *cham*, with rules laid down in the *cham-ying*, a sort of manual which is jealously guarded by the monks. The personages represented are deities and gurus (teachers) of the order to which the monastery belongs. Padmasambhava is one of the most popular: his peace-loving traits are portrayed by performers in monastic dress wearing masks with a serene expression, embodying the static aspect of mental

energy; at other times he is depicted as Guru Rinpoche, "The Precious Teacher", his head surmounted by five jewels symbolizing characteristics of the mind.

In some *cham* dances monks dressed in brocade and fur and armed with swords perform numerous leaps and acrobatic feats, intended to symbolize the spontaneous activity and the purity of a mind freed from ignorance. Although the monastic dances may vary in style and in the deities represented, they nearly always portray a struggle between the forces of good and evil, culminating with the ritual expulsion of evil, represented by a statuette made of plaster or clay (*linga*). The leading deity strikes it with the *purbha*, a dagger with three blades symbolizing consciousness, which cuts the knots of ignorance and thereby frees positive energy.

The intense emotional involvement felt by the audience is relieved by scenes of

comic relief provided by the grotesque *atsara*, clownish figures who may wear masks or have their faces covered in ashes or flour. They come rushing into the enclosure to joke with the spectators and perform farcical antics, delighting the Tibetans who have a strong sense of humor.

For the monks, *cham* is an important part of their Lamaist spiritual practices. Performing these dances combines deep meditation, intense mental concentration and a strong sense of visualization. By completely controlling mind and body, together with reciting the mantras of the particular deity personified, a monk succeeds in establishing a direct, personal relationship with the deity. At his most heightened state, the monk identifies with the god he is imitating.

After a long, grueling training, consisting of physical exercise and meditation every day, some dancers perform their role with such grace and harmony that their body is transfigured. They acquire a lightness that suggests spiritual elevation.

For the ordinary Tibetan people, *cham* performances are a profoundly religious experience as the dances bring them into contact with the most significant elements of their spiritual world. While they are watching the dances, the lay spectators are being taught sacred episodes from Buddhist history, as related in the ancient holy texts; and they are also becoming familiar with apparitions that they all are destined to encounter after death, and, by their mere presence, they gain many merits.

In the Nyimapa monastery of Katok actor-monks appear as deities who,
but for their animal heads, look like humans. On the following pages, the
structure of the temple in the background recalls that of Samg-dok-pel-ri,
dwelling-place of Guru Rinpoche.

Opposite, during cham *performed in the monastery at Zogqen, in Kham, this monk wears a characteristic headdress, shaped like a lotus. Above, a lama from the monastery in Labrang with a* tagdroma, *the hat typical of the Gelugpa (Yellow Hat) sect.*

The crowds which always throng these monastic dances participate body and soul in the celebration of the mysteries of their faith, to the point where the dividing line between real and unreal, human and divine, is dissolved. The deities portrayed by the actor-monks seem so genuine that, in the monastery courtyard, the audience sees only Yama, Mahakala, Padmasambhava and all the other deities made flesh and able to talk to human beings.

Tibet has always been considered a land of mystery, paranormal phenomena and the supernatural—a cradle of magic and occult lore. Its immense, empty landscapes, dominated by endless chains of mountains, its untamed beauty and the silence that accompanies the solitude of the wilds, make it an ideal place for superstitious belief in the supernatural to take root. Its fame as a land of mystery has been heightened by the tales of travelers who have crossed Tibet and met hermits, *Bön-po*, erudite lamas and *naldjorpa* (mystics).

Many apparently paranormal phenomena and amazing deeds attributed to supernatural powers can be partly explained—as Alexandra David-Néel herself pointed out—as the effects of mental training. Through concentration an extraordinary force can be developed which produces a form of energy. Certain ascetics have been known to survive the severest cold of the Tibetan winter clothed only in light cotton robes by practising *tumo*, a process of internal

self-heating, in which Alexandra David-Néel had herself been initiated. Others, like the *loung-gompa*, acquire supernatural lightness and speed and can run incredibly fast over very long distances.

According to Tibetan teachers, many phenomena stem from total control over mind and body, which can thus be freed of the passions, fears and egoism that block the path to Knowledge and Enlightenment. Alexandra David-Néel described Kham as "the seedbed of magic and witchcraft but also the home of Tibet's greatest intellectuals."[3] Her own, completely different cultural background encouraged her to find out all she could about the mysteries of Tibet. During periods spent in Kham and elsewhere in the eastern regions of the country she never missed an opportunity for making contact with hermits, learned lamas, miracle workers, mystics and

other experts in esoteric doctrines to increase her knowledge.

She was told of men who could see through mountains, or prevail over rain and hail; of magicians who practised rites like *rong lang*, the "corpse who stands up." The objective of this bizarre rite was to gain riches and magical powers. The magician had to embrace a corpse: physical contact and magic formulae were together supposed to transfuse it with the vital energy needed for resuscitation. At the first sign of life, the magician tore out the tongue which was transformed into a magic weapon.

On other occasions Alexandra David-Néel witnessed the hard tests to which disciples of the ascetics subjected themselves. One such practice was *chöd*: left alone at night in an isolated place likely to terrify the very bravest, the initiate had to free himself of all passions.

The pilgrims crowd forward to receive the lama's blessing, to be touched by his hands or by his dorje, and to be given water or tse ring rilbou, "pills of long life" (Katok, Kham).

*In dances depicting the fight of good against evil, the sword—tri —
metaphorically cuts the knots of ignorance and egoism; the three-bladed
dagger—purbha — is the symbol of consciousness that releases positive
energy (Monastery of Tsa Sa, Kham).*

155

The young monk then had destroy his consciousness of self by offering up his body as food for the demons he had summoned. Alexandra David-Néel, a lama herself and adept in certain rituals, was personally involved in strange and—to us—disturbing incidents such as the creation of a *tulpa*, or "phantom-being:" a creature formed by intense mental concentration and able, once provided with sufficient energy, to look and behave like a human. The *tulpa* has no mind of its own but is an empty form animated and directed by the magician who made it. It may, however, desire to be independent of its creator and to escape control.

A terrible struggle ensues, carried on by psychic means, and the creator may be so weakened as to lose his or her life-force. Alexandra David-Néel confirmed this: having succeeded in the difficult task of creating a *tulpa*, she struggled tremendously and at length to destroy it.

Over forty years of Chinese presence have certainly done much to alter the Tibet of the Gentlemen Brigands. And yet, in certain situations, visitors who do more than simply "pass through" the country or take what they see at face value will be surprised to rediscover, unchanged, the elements of Tibetan culture described by Alexandra David-Néel.

While we were in eastern Tibet, we often found ourselves experiencing the same feelings she described. In the dark, proud expression of a Golok, we read the life story of a gentleman brigand; mounted on the galloping horses of the Khampa we see the warriors of Gesar of Ling, launched in conquest of the kingdom of Hor. And if, on a winter evening, in the flickering light of an oil lamp, a blurred shadow appears by the entrance to a tent, we might find ourselves wondering whether it could be a rock-spirit, a demon or…a *tulpa*.

Above, a young tulku watches a cham *performed in Zogqen; opposite, a crowd of monks during* ser tren, *the devotional circumambulation. On the following pages,* cham *ritual dances are accompanied by the solemn sound of drums.*

NOTE: Many of the Tibetan words used in this book have been transcribed with the same transliteration used by Alexandra David-Néel herself, for instance *dokpa*. All the others have been transliterated phonetically.

The black-and-white photographs taken by Alexandra David-Néel come from the archives of the Fondation Alexandra David-Néel, Digne-les-Bains.

The map on page 13 is the work of Caterina Baratto, Nicoletta Gerlin and Elisabetta Gobbi.

SOURCES OF QUOTATIONS (see note on page 8)

Nomads of the Grassland Deserts
1. *Voyage d'une Parisienne à Lhassa*, Edition Plon, Paris 1929. Translated as *My Journey to Lhasa*, Harper and Bros , New York 1927
2. *A l'ouest barbare de la vaste Chine*, Edition Plon, Paris 1981
3. *A l'ouest barbare de la vaste Chine*, Edition Plon, Paris 1981
4. *A l'ouest barbare de la vaste Chine*, Edition Plon, Paris 1981
5. *Au pays des brigands gentilshommes*, Edition Plon, Paris 1933. Translated as *Tibetan Journey*, John Lane, London 1936
6. *Journal de voyage, lettres à son mari*, 2, Edition Plon, Paris 1975

The Sons of Gesar of Ling
1. *La vie surhumaine de Guésar de Ling*, Edition Di Rochet, Paris 1931. Translated as *The Superhuman Life of Gesar of Ling*, London, Rider & Co. 1933
2. *Au pays des brigands gentilshommes*, Edition Plon, Paris 1933
3. *Au pays des brigands gentilshommes*, Edition Plon, Paris 1933
4. *Journal de voyage, lettres à son mari*, 2, Edition Plon, Paris 1975
5. *Au pays des brigands gentilshommes*, Edition Plon, Paris 1933
6. *Journal de voyage, lettres à son mari*, 2, Edition Plon, Paris 1975
7. *Journal de voyage, lettres à son mari*, 2, Edition Plon, Paris 1975

Horses of the Wind
1. *Voyage d'une Parisienne à Lhassa*, Edition Plon, Paris 1929
2. *Au pays des brigands gentilshommes*, Edition Plon, Paris 1933
3. *Mystiques et magiciens*, Edition Plon, Paris 1929. Translated as *With Mystics and Magicians in Tibet*, London, John Lane 1931

Winter in the Land of Snows
1. *Journal de voyage, lettres à son mari*, 2, Edition Plon, Paris 1975
2. *A l'ouest barbare de la vaste Chine*, Edition Plon, Paris 1981
3. *Voyage d'une Parisienne à Lhassa*, Edition Plon, Paris 1929
4. *Voyage d'une Parisienne à Lhassa*, Edition Plon, Paris 1929
5. *Au pays des Brigands gentilshommes*, Edition Plon, Paris 1933
6. *A l'ouest barbare de la vaste Chine*, Edition Plon, Paris 1981

In the Valleys of the Gyarongpas
1. *Au pays des Brigands gentilshommes*, Edition Plon, Paris 1933
2. *Au pays des Brigands gentilshommes*, Edition Plon, Paris 1933
3. *Journal de voyage, lettres à son mari*, 2, Edition Plon, Paris 1975

Mysteries of Tibet
1. *Journal de voyage, lettres à son mari*, 2, Edition Plon, Paris 1975
2. *Journal de voyage, lettres à son mari*, 2, Edition Plon, Paris 1975
3. *A l'ouest barbare de la vaste Chine*, Edition Plon, Paris 1981